History of t
Miniature ⸝⸝y

A pioneering 7¼ inch gauge garden railway
built in the grounds of Kenton Grange

Jeffress Family	-	Kenton Grange
The Railway	-	1931 to 1950
The Locomotives	-	1931 to 2015

Eric L Basire

History of the Kenton Miniature Railway

Henry Greenly drives the 4-4-0 "George V" locomotive on the KMR with one of the engineers (Jackson?) as passenger. This may be the very first visit by HG. Note the early post-and-beam track.

ISBN – 13: 978-1514189986

Printed by Create Space

Jeffress approaches the KMR station driving his "Royal Scot" (c 1948)

The author driving the ex-KMR "Royal Scot" at the Ascot Locomotive Society track 1994

My link to this brief history of an important pioneering miniature garden railway started when, as a young teenager, I visited the KMR and took a ride. Randolph Jeffress built his railway with the help of his friend Henry Greenly who also designed the locomotives.

Above are two pictures which epitomise my interest to find out as much as possible about the owner, his railway and the locomotives. I wanted to know if the locomotives were still in service and to see if I could actually view them. With the Royal Scot I went one step further, during the Henry Greenly Rally held at the Ascot Locomotive Society in 1994, I was allowed to drive it! Dorset 2015

Kenton Miniature Railway

FOREWORD

January 1996 marked the Golden Anniversary of the Harrow and Wembley Society of Model Engineers and as part of the celebrations I decided to write the Club's history. The Society holds a notable position in the national model engineering scene and I thought it was important to record details of past achievements of the club and its many well-known members.

Thus in 1993 I started researching information for the club history. I discovered that the first raised test running track was built in the grounds of the Grange, Kenton, Middlesex. This discovery brought back personal memories of visits I had made in my teens to the Kenton Miniature Railway which ran round the garden of the Grange. My last visit to the KMR was on a rare running day not long before it closed in 1949. It was interesting to recall that I did not see the Harrow and Wembley Society track but it may have already been dismantled, or just simply hidden in the undergrowth.

Thus I became side-tracked into trying to find out what happened to the KMR and the seven locomotives which operated on the line. It took two years to complete my research and my short history was privately published in 1995. (I did also manage to complete a club history.)

The local reaction was very good and I have made many interesting contacts, not the least being Mr George Wells, a local professional photographer. He was a close friend of Mr Joseph Jeffress the owner of the Grange. Mr Wells gave me his striking photo of Mr Jeffress which features on the cover of my book.

In my early first edition I suggested that there was more to be discovered and this has been proved to be correct. In this expanded history I can relate more about this interesting part of Harrow's history which I hope will provide a valuable insight into the Jeffress Family, the Kenton Miniature Railway and the Locomotives. In 2005 I managed to trace information about one of the seven locomotives which was missing. It had been exported to North America and I can now include it as part of the story. Of the additional information gathered at this time some produced coincidences which connect me with the story of the railway.

My special thanks to my friends Peter Newbrook and David Robinson, to Jack Newbutt and his son Michael and Joe Carroll. Also Rob and Steven

Foxon, Geoffrey Holme, Joe Holman, Mr H Bowtell, Mr L Busby, Mr G Wells, Mr C Finken, Ms H Simpson, Mr J Lawes, the Wembley Historical Society and the present owners of the KMR locomotives.

A critical contact has been Michael Newbutt, son of Jack, and we have become friends by exchanging valuable information. Mike spent part of his childhood at Kenton Grange when his father was the KMR Engineer. As a result of this correspondence Michael has generously agreed to let me use a whole selection of photographs which add much to the history. He has also provided some new anecdotes about his family's links with the KMR. Some photos have been used to improve pictures within the text but the majority now form a photo album at the end of the book. Some photos were taken with basic box cameras and they are included for their historical interest.

In 2000 I moved to Dorset. I remain a member of the Harrow & Wembley Society but have found an equally fine club in the Wimborne & District Society of Model Engineers.

During the last twenty years I have had many requests for copies of my history which I published privately on my PC. The individual stories of the seven ex-KMR locomotives have continued through time. Perhaps 2030, the 100th anniversary of the start of the KMR, would be a good time to publish but I have new stories to tell and it seems now is a good time to see if I can get my efforts published.

Now, with new information and photos, some twenty years after the first edition, I offer this revised and expanded history.

Eric L Basire
West Moors
May 2015

History of Kenton Miniature Railway

CONTENTS

History of Kenton Miniature Railway

CHAPTER 1

INTRODUCTION

This is the story of the Kenton Miniature Railway, built in the garden of a small manor house. It also includes stories of the Jeffress family and follows the seven locomotives which were constructed to work on the railway.

In the 1930s there was an exchange of letters in the Model Engineering magazine about the best gauge for miniature garden railways which were becoming popular. One letter from W J Bassett-Lowke, the well-known miniature locomotive manufacturer, added this to the debate:-

"Mr Jeffress, of Kenton Grange, who has one of the largest collections of 7¼ in. locomotives in the country, finds that this gauge excellently fulfils his garden railway requirements on the comprehensive line he is laying."

With his friend Henry Greenly as guide and designer it is reasonable to view Randolph Jeffress' KMR as one of the leaders in the development of miniature garden railways at the time.

While researching information for my history of my club, the Harrow & Wembley Society of Model Engineers (HWSME), I became side-tracked by the Kenton Miniature Railway (KMR). In 1939 the HWSME obtained permission from the KMR owner Mr Jeffress to erect their first raised test track in his garden at Kenton Grange. The Society regularly used this facility until 1949 when the imminent sale of the Grange was announced.

In my search for information about the KMR I found two reports in back issues of the Model Engineer [1] by Henry Greenly. He was able to entitle his second report 'Kenton Miniature Railway Re-visited'. The railway ceased in 1949/50 so I am unable to write having recently visited the KMR. I can only produce a retrospective review of this interesting 7¼" gauge railway and what items survive to the present day.

---

[1]   *"An American 'Pacific' Model for 7¼ inch Gauge"* Model Engineer 4th Jan 1934 (page3)
    "Kenton Miniature Railway Re-visited" Model Engineer 16th March 1939 (page314)

The information sources for this history came from many people and documents, some of which provided conflicting details. It was, therefore, necessary to take a careful balance of all the information to produce a history which, as far as possible, was confirmed from other records.

Here are two very early photographs to set the scene. The KMR owner Randolph Jeffress in between his railway engineer Mr E Roberts (left) and his friend the famous loco designer Henry Greenly (right). The second picture is of the steam raising area of the Harrow & Wembley SME. Many of the photographs in this book were taken with simple box cameras and quality suffers. They are, however, of historic interest.

Left to right: Roberts, Jeffress and Greenly   Vacuum used to raise steam on HWSME track

'The Grange' Kenton Road, Kenton, Middlesex, is a long established manor house originally with extensive grounds of about 27 acres. Built by John Lambert in the early 19th century it included two lakes, two lodge houses and two cottages. Apart from the Grange itself one lodge and the two cottages still exist in Woodgrange Ave. The frontage onto Kenton Road stretches from Gooseacre Lane in the east to Woodgrange Ave in the west. In 1915 the house was purchased by Mr Albert Gustavus Jeffress, wealthy American from Virginia.

Today the Grange is owned by St Luke's Hospice serving the Greater London Boroughs of Brent and Harrow. The remaining area of garden consists mainly of the original lawn area at the back of the house. It is still possible to trace, in the open public ground south of the house, some of the line taken by the track along the southern embankment.

2

CHAPTER 2

THE JEFFRESS FAMILY

Albert Gustavus Jeffress

Albert Jeffress, Deputy Chairman of British-American Tobacco, purchased Kenton Grange in 1915. He died unexpectedly of a heart attack just before Christmas1925 while on board ship returning from a trip to the Far East. Unfortunately, Albert's death seems to have resulted in a series of life-long mental problems for his widow Stella Adelaide. His eldest son Joseph Randolph took over as head of the family. Everyone locally and those linked directly to the railway thought he was the only child. Although there were a few rumours of another son his existence was never acknowledge.

Shortly after publication of the first edition of this history I established a close contact with St Luke's Hospice. This local organisation owned a building in central Harrow and had ambitious plans to buy the Grange and convert it as a residential hospice. On a number of occasions the Harrow & Wembley SME donated a day's takings to St Luke's who also set up a fund raising stall. The hospice eventually raised sufficient funds and achieved their aims by purchasing the Grange from Brent Council.

In 1996 Leslie Dodd, my main contact with the Grange Hospice project, phoned to tell me that Helen Simpson, from Southampton Art Museum, was interested in the Jeffress family and would be visiting the Grange. She asked if she could pass on my name as someone who had information but instead I suggested a meeting with Helen during her visit to Kenton.

Helen's interest came through a generous bequest from Arthur Tilden Jeffress who gave a hundred paintings to the Southampton Art Museum. This provided a lasting and very valuable collection of artwork for a local art gallery.

After talking at the Grange Helen and I went to Harrow School where we were given access to records on both Randolph Jeffress and his younger brother Arthur. After further research it transpired the younger brother may have been the family's 'black sheep' who left home to pursue his own very successful path in life. He became very well known and a wealthy art collector and dealer.

Arthur Tilden Jeffress

This part of the story diverts from the Grange and the railway. Arthur developed a very successful art dealership with a gallery 'Arthur Jeffress Pictures' near London's Hanover Square. He was a well connected figure in the art world and the Southampton Gallery has a portrait of him by his long term friend the artist Grahame Sutherland.

Arthur lived for a while at Marwell House, about 9 miles from Southampton, and supported the local Gallery by the loan of paintings for exhibition. He also had a very elegant apartamento (almost a mini palazzo) in Venice. His personal gondola had white and gold suited gondoliers

Detail from Grahame Sutherland's painting of Arthur Jeffress. Southampton Art Gallery

Many years ago I converted the well known Airfix Kitmaster "00" plastic locomotive kits into fully working models. One of my regular customers was Peter Newbrook a film director. We became good friends and when I sent him an early copy of the KMR history he replied with an amazing coincidence. In the early part of his career he worked on a film directed by David Lean called 'Summer Madness' starring Katherine Hepburn and Rossano Brazzi. The film was shot entirely on location in Venice. Members of the film company were often guests at the American artist Peggy Guggenheim's palazzo and another regular guest was Arthur Jeffress. There were subsequent invitations from Arthur to amazing parties held in his apartment.

Peter remembered *"The food and wine served beggared description. Several times after dinner, I was asked if I would like to stay behind, but having been tipped off, I gracefully declined and in due time the invitations ceased"*. He went on to report *"However, the real trouble was drugs and every possible variety was available. Unfortunately, one member of the film company became hooked and did not work for several years until he managed to clean himself up"*. Peter concluded, *"Drugs have never appealed to me and I wasn't*

4

bothered by homosexuals - I had worked with gay actors all my life!".

This story has a sad end. When leaving a dinner party at Arthur's the Duchess of Windsor asked if she could use his gondola. Unfortunately, the gondoliers could not be found and Arthur was furious. Although he did not sack them he was said to be considering buying a motor boat. There was a Police purge in Venice on homosexuals at the time. Whether the gondoliers struck back by informing the authorities of the goings on by their employer, or if word simply got out, we don't know. When Arthur returned from a holiday in Corfu, he was not allowed to enter Venice on pain of arrest. Friends got him aboard a train for England but on an overnight stop in Paris he apparently committed suicide with an overdose of drugs.

In his Will he left one hundred paintings to the Southampton Art Gallery. The Curator was allowed to select those he wanted from the collection. Most of the paintings were in Venice and had to be rescued before being damaged by the damp or stolen by vandals. Today this collection forms the foundation for one of the few regional galleries to own a highly valuable and notable collection.

Joseph Randolph Jeffress

Recent evidence indicates Joseph preferred his second name Randolph. He was a man of many interests but his main hobbies revolved around fast cars, photography and his miniature railway. The workshops at the Grange are set apart from the main house in an old stable block. The block forms a square around an open courtyard and over the arched entrance is a clock tower. In the late 1920s racing cars, mainly at Brooklands famous race track, were Randolph's main hobby.

He employed Frank Elsden as a mechanic to maintain the cars. Frank initially lived in Harrow but in 1928/9 he and his family moved into Clock Cottage which is situated next to the entrance into the old stable yard of Kenton Grange. Shortly after this Randolph rolled over one of his cars on the steep banking at Brooklands. When getting out and rather shaken he reported to say "You know, I think we're getting rather too old for this Elsden". In 1930 racing motor cars was given up to concentrate on the building of the garden railway. Frank's engineering expertise was retained and two other engineers employed to construct the locomotives, the railway and running stock. Mr E Roberts was appointed as chief engineer assisted by Mr Jackson. In his article about the

American locomotive, in the ME magazine 1934, Henry Greenly mentions engineer Roberts. He included a photograph which is reproduced in chapter one of this book [page 2]. Although some cars were retained work on servicing them surely reduced when racing was abandoned. Frank's workload must have also lessened and there is no doubt his engineering skills were important in helping to establish and run the railway. For example we know he spent time cutting by hand the mainframes for locos out of large sheets of steel. The right hand side (west) of the stable block was the original workshop for cars but this was converted into the storage and workshop for the railway and a new access to the track was provided by a small door in the back wall.

Frank Elsden (standing) at the KMR station with two trains pulled by 'Flying Scotsman' and 'Hudson' locos. On the top right Randolph is taking a ride. Photo D Elsden

Randolph's interest in photography was mainly concerned with very early colour photographs. A local enthusiast George Wells provided much of the technical skills and Jeffress covered the expenditure. One of their earliest cameras has been passed on to the national museum collection of historic cameras. Also there is one of their best early colour photos 'The Girl in Pink' produced by Randolph and George. During the production of this photo the two became obsessed with reproducing the exact shade of pink dress which a young girl modelled sitting at a grand piano in the Grange. As each

6

experimental camera fell out of use it was stored away. Later George set up his own photographic business close by in Kenton Road taking formal family photographs.

Around 1930 Randolph became interested in garden railways and decided locomotives with 7¼" gauge were to be used. It is not known if he knew or consulted Henry Greenly about his plans. However, Henry was to play an important part in the KMR. The first locomotive to arrive at Kenton was a Great Central Railway 4-6-0 'Immingham' Class designed by Greenly. Full details of this loco later. The photo on the page opposite my introduction at the start of this book shows Henry driving the 4-4-0 'George the Fifth' at Kenton. He was visiting when this early model, completed at Kenton in 1932, was running. It also shows the original post and beam track construction which may have caused problems in later years. Later we will discover Henry's suggested design for the renewal of the track so it could cope with bigger, heavier locomotives and passenger trains.

Jack and Michael Newbutt

Before moving onto the details of the railway it seems sensible to relate here some of the story provided by Michael Newbutt. He spent some of his early childhood at Kenton Grange when his father Jack moved into the Grange's London Lodge House fronting on Kenton Road. Additional information about the subsequent history of the Newbutts and three of the KMR locos has been added later in this record. Michael contacted me to obtain a copy of my KMR history in December 2007. I sent a copy of the second edition to him and these are some of his reactions. They give another dimension to Randolph Jeffress with whom he came into regular contact.

"The picture of Joseph on the cover immediately invoked memories of him. I was only eight when we left Kenton and he was always kind to me and this is the first proper picture I have seen of him since. I well remember him driving down the bendy drive in some noisy car and having to avoid me playing, but he always had a smile and a wave."

[On page 12 is the drawing which Michael now refers to]

"The superimposed drawing of the railway on the new developments is interesting. The railway certainly went over the pond, I remember being told to look out for duck's eggs floating on the water as we went across.

"The raised track of the HWSME (on the) drawing brought back some memories. I had been given, by Joseph, an 'O' gauge Basset-Lowke 2-6-0 spirit fired tender loco which I think at the time were mass produced and came in various guises. It just so happened that, give or take 1/32' or so,'O' gauge fitted the difference between two of the multi gauge rails on that track so I spent many happy hours with the whole track to myself but with lots of derailments, burnt fingers and invaluable experience."

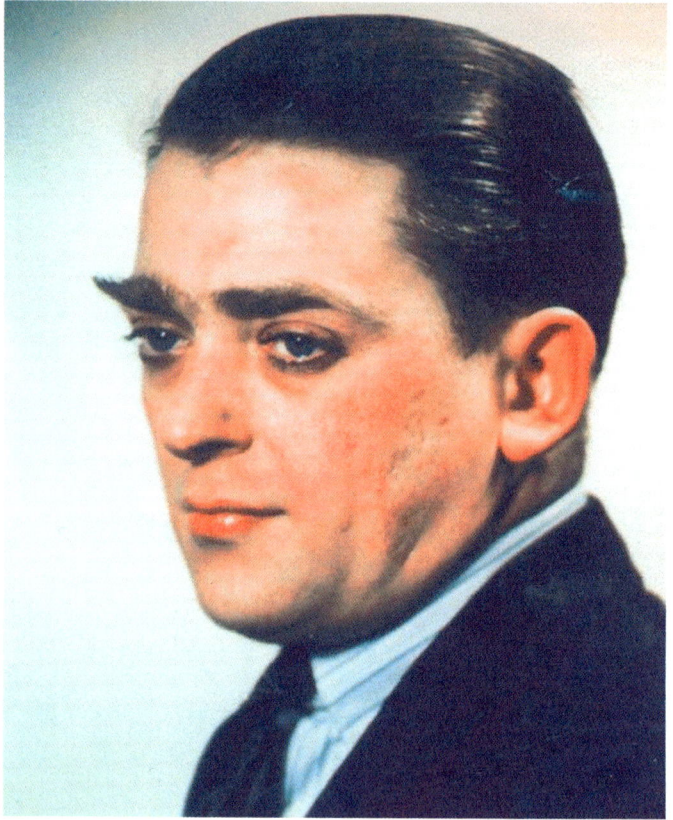

Jack Newbutt taken with a camera he built with Randolph & George's help.

Every small boy's dream – Michael with his dad Jack and the 'Hudson' loco

Michael Newbutt reunited with the 'Royal Scot' in the summer 2008 at the Spinney Light Railway

History of the Kenton Miniature Railway

CHAPTER 3

THE RAILWAY 1931 – 1950

By the 1930's much of the Grange's original 27 acres had been sold for housing including a large open area used for Woodcock Hill Park. The few acres of garden were all that remained. As mentioned above, Randolph Jeffress was, like many wealthy men of his time, interested in cars and he developed a comprehensive workshop facility in the old stable buildings. Randolph's enthusiasm turned to garden railways and he developed his workshops for building and storage of 7¼" gauge live steam locomotives.

The first works manager was Mr E Roberts who, assisted by Mr Jackson, and Frank Elsden built the railway, the first locomotives and the rolling stock. Randolph's American background gave him an interest in models of USA types of locomotives. This was to create some unique models in the early days of model engineering when model engineers usually based their efforts on British prototypes or freelance designs.

The single line track ran for about two thirds of a mile around the main garden area to the south of the house. A passing loop was provided through the station which was at the furthest point from the house. Starting at the station and taking a clock-wise trip :- the line ran west on a low embankment *[the general slope of the ground is from north to south]* turning to the north in a long curve. Next came the tunnel and then, as it emerged, the track turned east across the lawns in a shallow cutting. It then passed under a footbridge and over the pond into the area behind the workshop. Running alongside the turntable, which provided access to the workshops, the line took a long gentle curve south to reach the station. It is still possible to trace the line of the embankment but the cutting has long disappeared.

A drawing of the railway

The drawing on the next page was created by superimposing the KMR and the Harrow & Wembley SME raised tracks on a modern map of the area. This was carried out by Brent Council staff using an old aerial view of the Grange. However, from my own visit when the railway was operating the trains ran over the pond, which others have confirmed including Michael Newbutt. Now I also have photographic evidence showing the track running closer to the garden wall (green line) and the back of the workshop. I have added a red broken line showing where we believe the Main line ran. In 1995 the empty pond showed evidence of the central pier of a bridge.

There was a tunnel made from an old farm building with the end walls removed, just as the line entered the cutting which ran across the lawn. At the southern end was a 'jungle' of foliage which extended the tunnel effect. The approximate location of the tunnel is shown on the map. Today it is still possible to trace the embankment through the trees in the public open area at the bottom left of the drawing. 'Clock Cottage' is at the top right corner of the Workshop building.

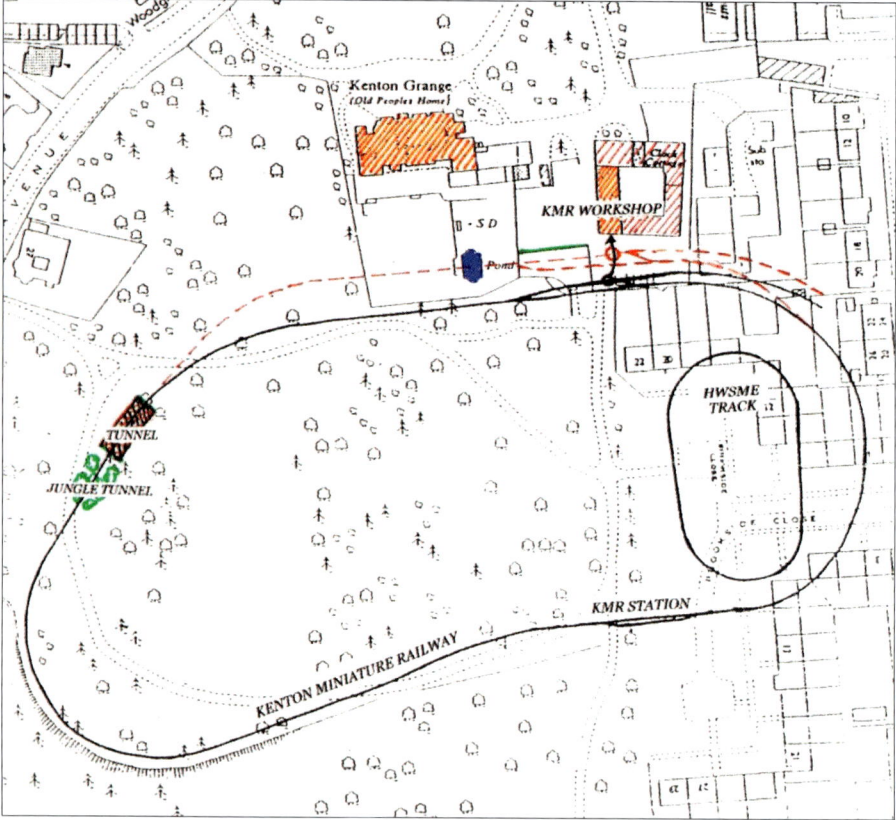

The Station

The following two photographs of the station show the passing loop. The first is a copy of a postcard and shows a west-bound train entering a busy platform. Randolph Is in charge of 'Immingham' with the train heavily loaded with children. Trains never ran in both directions on the same day. However, they did run in opposite directions on alternate open days to even out wear on

The Station, Kenton Miniature Railway, Kenton, Middlesex

the wheel flanges. The station, built from an ex-WD hut, had two rooms. The main waiting room had a separate storage area at the back. At the western end (behind the photographer) a point provided an access line to the rear store through a low door where locos were taken if it rained. Randolph was reportedly very concerned if they got wet. Between the rails inside the hut was an old enamelled advertisement which protected the wooden floor from the hot cinders. Steaming up was often done at the station using materials from the store. I have not managed to find any photographic evidence of the junction leading into this facility.

[When I visited the railway in 1949 not long before closure the station building had already gone and the passing loop lay in long grass. The area was still being used as the passenger station. Author]

13

At a later date – the central platform has disappeared. Here we see an eastbound train with No7 American 'Hudson' locomotive. As this loco was built in 1947 this photo must have been taken after that date.

TheTrack

In his 'Model Engineer' article on The American Pacific loco Henry Greenly mentions his meeting with Randolph Jeffress at a 'Model Engineer' exhibition when their conversation turned to modelling American locos for the KMR. This may have been the first time they met. The article was written in 1933 after the loco in question had been completed. When the two had their conversation 'Immingham' was at Kenton and 'George the Fifth' was recently completed. 'Flying Scotsman' was under construction and all three locos were designed by Greenly so he was aware of their weight limits.

A crash – what was the cause?

Clearly shown in this photo of the crash is the early 'post and beam' type of support used for most of the line and although derailments were few they were always feared. Not long after the 'NYC Pacific' loco was complete it was involved in a serious derailment when it left the track at speed and Randolph was badly injured. Although speed was involved the early track design was also suspect. Henry believed that *"Where children are among the passengers on a narrow track they often act thoughtlessly and care in construction details is essential."*

The initial track was lightly built and Henry realised that the heavy USA model would have to be carefully designed to closely match the wheel loading of the British models already running. Greenly lived in Heston, about seven miles from Kenton and after the accident the two friends worked closely on the development of the railway.

Greenly advised the line should be levelled with embankments and cuttings to ensure the track was laid on solid ground. The new track was laid with 9lb per yard flat-bottomed steel rail tied with pressed corrugated steel sleepers in ballast. He calculated scale sleepers laid in ballast would only support 30lb per axle on a typical two seat passenger coach. In fact with two adult passengers per truck at Kenton the loading often exceeded 100lb. Over-scale sleepers were essential for safe running of the line and an occasional heavy wooden sleeper was included to add stability. The innovative point-work was designed at Kenton and involved the use of cast frogs with pivoted supports for the rail. The frogs were complete with wings and when worn the ends were replaced with steel screwed to the plate. The point rails were formed from standard mild steel flats 2' x ½' which were bonded together by long bolts to prevent them overturning. This saved the problem of forming point blades from flat-bottomed rail. Slide chairs were not required and pieces of flat plate were used to support the sliding point rails.

15

Originally the Kenton Miniature Railway was entirely private but in the late thirties it was opened to the public on limited days. Rides were free but it became so popular a small charge was introduced - if anything this seems to have increased the number visiting every Saturday afternoon. All profits were donated to local charities and in particular Wembley Hospital. On busy days there were three locomotives in steam. An ex-resident of Kenton, Mr L Busby, remembers a very large sign on the Kenton Road advertising the railway which directed visitors to walk along to Gooseacre Lane to gain access to the station. Shortly after the sign was erected London Transport placed a new bus stop for the 183 route so passengers could visit the Grange. The sign was taken away during WW2. Another local contemporary was at school with Randolph's son Godfrey. The lad was invited by Godfrey to visit the Grange after school *"To see my trains."* He expected a Hornby '00' layout but found himself in the garden viewing a large railway.

The Rolling Stock

The construction of locomotives was the main activity for the engineers working at Kenton. In addition to this and the work maintaining the track there was the ongoing provision of rolling stock. This was mainly in the form of passenger cars for all sizes of children and adults. All the stock was built at Kenton Works. Early scale four-wheel trucks were developed into bogie and articulated vehicles. These eventually had their body dimensions increased in width and length to provide more room. There were ten of these three-car sets each capable of carrying six adults. Simple blocks of wood were used for buffers which eliminated the problem of locking.

This photo shows one of the early trucks. The boy is probably Randolph's son Godfrey. Bogies developed into this USA pattern. Some trucks were later turned into articulated sets of three or five carriages.

The bogie.

Completed 7¼ in. gauge truck made by Mr. J. R. Jeffress.

This later style of passenger car was of a 'garden seat' pattern (see photo opposite)

16

Ex KMR articulated "Garden seat" style coaches at Coniston Railway   Photo D Robinson

It is possible that the earlier trucks were converted into this open version since they provided more room for the passengers - especially the adults. Many of the surviving photographs show trains made up of three or five articulated 'garden seat' cars. A number of these sets survive to-day and are located on railways where the ex-KMR locos still run. This photo is one of the best examples and shows the ex-Kenton cars when at Coniston.

Other rolling stock on the KMR included a sanding truck, a set of hopper wagons for ballasting and a single enclosed passenger car. This roofed vehicle was nicknamed the 'Honeymoon coach'. It was placed at the end of a train, usually with an unsuspecting young lady as the second occupant. As the train passed through the tunnel it was 'slipped' to leave the passengers trapped inside until the next train arrived to push it out.

A busy year - 1939

In 1939 members from the Harrow & Wembley Society of Model Engineers obtained permission to build a club track in Mr Jeffress' garden. Members regularly walked down behind the workshop to cross the KMR tracks to reach their railway hut. Committee meetings were held under the clock tower in a room over the archway. They paid their landlord the sum of £1.05p (one guinea) per annum for this privilege. Randolph was President of the Society

17

for a few years and no doubt found an interest in the models running on the raised track. Then the storm clouds gathered and World War II started. In his ME article of March 1939 Henry Greenly reports that Elsden was in charge of the Works. There is no information as to the departure of Messrs Roberts and Jackson but the threat of war was a concern for everyone.

War Years

There is little information about what happened during the second World War. As mentioned above Frank Elsden was in charge of the workshops. Around the beginning of 1941 he moved his family to Bridgewater, Somerset. Frank was working for a company which evacuated wholesale with all employees out of the dangers of bombing in London. The facts that Frank was employed elsewhere, and Roberts and Jackson had left, may have been the result of financial problems. In any case the partial closure of the railway due to wartime restrictions reduced the need for a threesome workshop team.

Local sources suggest there was little activity because of some minor local opposition concerning the 'waste of coal' when families were having a hard time obtaining fuel for use in their homes. The fact that the proceeds from running were donated to charity may have been a factor in allowing the railway to operate from time to time. An alternative view from a regular volunteer John Lawes who suggests during the war years the railway continued to run frequently as part of a Government 'Holidays at Home' campaign. It helped to entertain the local population. As a result the use of some coal was officially sanctioned.

An Auxiliary Fire Service station had an entrance in Woodgrange Avenue and Randolph allowed the firemen to set up allotments in his garden. They even kept chickens in a very large coop. A wooden bridge over the line from Gooseacre Lane was provided for the allotment holders but most walked over the track which was also used to scrape the mud from their boots and spades. Some allotments were inside the Harrow & Wembley Society of Model Engineer's oval of raised track which also suffered from mud cleaning.

CHAPTER 4

THE LOCOMOTIVES

There is some confusion about the sequence in which the locomotives were acquired/built at Kenton. The numbering does not help. For example the American locos were numbered after the year in which they were constructed. The New York Central 4-6-2 built in 1933 was 'NYC1933'. Some of the other locomotives did not follow this pattern. To simplify this problem the list produced by Henry Greenly for his article in the 'Model Engineer' in 1939 will be used in this record.

In addition to this 'official list' two other engines have been mentioned as regulars on the track. They were a 'Single-wheeler' and a Great Eastern 4-4-0 'Claud Hamilton Class'. This latter may have been an error for KMR No 2 'George the Fifth' but it could have been an early loco kept in the workshop which was in a bad condition and never ventured out. This GER loco might be the subject of the rebuild as a Highland Railway 4-4-0 [see the drawing later – 'The loco that never was?'] Perhaps, these models may have been owned by friends of Jeffress, or locals, who are mentioned to have run at the KMR on a regular basis. Alternatively, they may have been earlier purchases which were subsequently sold. The possibility there were two earlier locos is supported by a postcard which shows No 1 'Immingham' but is entitled 'Kenton Miniature Railway No 3 Engine'.

Postcard: Kenton Miniature Railway No 3 Engine

19

Henry's article listed seven locomotives, completed or planned. All, with the exception of No 1, were either built or finished in the Kenton Works. Greenly designed all and various manufacturers supplied castings, parts, or part built engines. Randolph's preference was for slide valves so all locos included this feature. In 1939 a large 4-8-4 type American loco was nearing completion which would supplement the five in running condition at the time. Greenly's KMR stock list was as follows:

No 1:   Great Central Railway 4-6-0 'Immingham Class'.

No 2:   London & North Western Railway 4-4-0 'George the Fifth'.

No 3:   'NYC1933 American Pacific' 4-6-2 (small New York Central type)

No 4:   LNER Pacific 4-6-2 'Flying Scotsman'.

No 5:   LMS 4-6-0 'Royal Scot'.

No 6:   No 1939 American 4-8-4 'Northern' with 12 wheel tender.

No 7:   No 1947 American 4-6-4 'Hudson' Express locomotive.

Now, that a list of all seven locos was available to work from, it was time to see if the any of them still existed and, if they did, what sort of condition would they be in?

No 1: **Great Central Railway 4-6-0 'Immingham' Class**

Built by Bassett-Lowke of Northampton in 1908 it was modelled by Henry Greenly on one of J G Robinson's successful express engines of 1906. The loco was commissioned by Mr Ernest Coats (owner of Coats Cotton Reels fame). This was their first 7¼' gauge locomotive and led to other models in the same scale designed as moderately priced motive power for garden railways.

In 1908 the Society of Model Experimental Engineers visited the Bassett-Lowke works where 'Immingham' was undergoing steam trials. The model has 1⅞' x 3' cylinders and driving wheels 9¾' diameter.

There is a report which suggests Mr Coats declined to pay for the completed engine until it had been inspected by two independent gentlemen. One was J G Robinson, the designer of the prototype, and the other Sir Aubrey Brocklebank who later featured in many Bassett-Lowke publications driving 'Immingham'. The price was £250, a large sum of money at the start of the century. In addition Mr Coats purchased two or more four-wheeled trucks each with a recessed foot well marked with the initials 'ESC'

'Immingham' vanished until it was overhauled by H S C Bullock and offered for sale at £100 in 1931. It was then Randolph Jeffress purchased it for the Kenton Miniature Railway.

This faded newspaper photo shows the KMR 'Royal Scot' and 'Immingham', then 40 years old, at the start of the 1948 running season. Taken in the station area where the platforms and building had already been removed.

When the KMR closed in1949 the locomotive was sold to Sir John Samuel and ran on his Greywood Central Railway, Walton-upon-Thames. Very finely painted and lined out with 'Greywood Central' on the tender the loco was much admired. Visitors to the line, including Walt Disney **and railway artist Terence Cuneo had a** turn at driving her.

'Immingham' on the Greywood Central Railway   Photo B Wright

There is no record of when the loco was sold and left Greywood Central but Terence Holder owned her until it was purchased by John Crawley around 1965. Finally the loco passed on to Christopher Finken where the last information was that, over 90 years old 'Immingham' was again requiring another substantial overhaul. As Christopher suggests – *"In many ways 'Immingham' is the archetypal Edwardian engine, certainly capturing the atmosphere of pre-grouping livery splendour, with an elegance that has appealed to many over the years."*

21

No 2: **London & North Western Railway 4-4-0 'George the Fifth'**

The prototype locomotive was first introduced in 1909 at Crewe under the direction of C J Bowen-Cooke. Some years later Bassett-Lowke decided to include a model in their 'not too expensive' garden railway series. The castings and drawings were purchased and this became the first KMR engine to be completely built in their own workshops at Kenton. While Messrs Roberts, Jackson and Elsden were constructing the 'George V' they also started work on the LNER 'Flying Scotsman' 4-6-2 Pacific. The 'George' was completed in 1932.

After Kenton it is possible the loco was purchased by Raymond Marks in 1949/50. It eventually found its way to the private Spinney Railway. It passed, on the owner J Ballentyne-Dykes' death, to his son who had it re-built in L&NWR black livery. In 2010 the loco is still at the Spinney Light Railway and once again is in need of some tlc.

'George Vth' on the Spinney Railway
[Driver John Raymond friend of J Ballantyne-Dykes]

'George V' at the Spinney Light Railway in 2002
            Photo: D Robinson

22

No 3: **American New York Central 'Pacific' 4-6-2 NYC1933**

In 1932 the Kenton Works' team was constructing No 4 'Flying Scotsman'. After discussing with Randolph the production of an American type 4-6-2 locomotive in 7¼" gauge for the KMR Greenly realised the finished model would have to meet the weight limits of the track at Kenton. Using many of the drawings and castings for the 4-6-2 'Flying Scotsman' Henry designed a NYC loco for Randolph's team to construct. It is possible that Jeffress' enthusiasm to have an American model resulted in a change of priority over the current construction of the LNER 'Pacific' which appears to have been put on hold..

The 'NYC' was completed first in 1933. However, even with Greenly's careful design the engine left the post and beam track at speed and, as recorded earlier, Randolph was badly injured and the track subsequently rebuilt. 'NYC 1933' featured in Greenly's 'Model Engineer' article published on 4th January 1934.

The following photograph of the completed 'NYC1933' 4-6-2 shows the skills of the designer and the team at Kenton. The loco stands on the turntable at the back of the workshops.

Henry Greenly's 1934 'ME' article gives many details of this unique locomotive. The two men met at a 'ME' Exhibition and discussed design and construction of a freelance 1½" scale 'Pacific' for the KMR. The 'George V' was up and running but Randolph wanted something more powerful. Apart from minor details the basic design and scale was the same as the LNER 'Pacific' which was already being built at Kenton. By special request slide valves were incorporated. To simplify construction, and to make the valve's hanger centers interchangeable with Greenly's standard double ported piston valve cylinders, the combination lever was attached at the top to a special form of crosshead guide supported from the valve gear girder frame. The lug on this guide was attached to the valve spindle by fore-and-aft nuts, thus the final valve adjustment could be made even when in steam. The boiler was made of 9" dia solid drawn copper tube with riveted and fullered joints. The final caulking being soft solder of 'aircraft quality'. There were 47 tubes. Greenly's 1903 pattern regulator was used which was a disc valve arranged in a tube within the barrel of the boiler. It could easily be withdraw for servicing. The firebox was fitted to the frame by Mr H Ivatts' (GNR) design of a flexible expansion holding plate.

Mr E H Roberts (KMR Engineer) has been responsible for nine-tenths of the work. Mr Jeffress took every interest in the details of the work during the construction and recorded much of it with his excellent home cine camera. A very short piece of film showing running at Kenton is included on Railfilms DVD 'Miniature Line Memories'.

1940s Line-up left to right:' NYC1933'; 4-8-4 'Northern'; 'Royal Scot' and many junior helpers!

No 4: **London North Eastern Railway 4-6-2 'Flying Scotsman'**

In terms of sequence this Greenly designed 'Flying Scotsman' was under construction before No 3. However, the anticipation of an American loco for KMR may have put this one on the 'back burner'. Mr Jeffress had stated that he intended to build one new locomotive every year and he tried to standardise many of the parts in his stud of engines.

After the 'NYC Pacific' in 1933 this loco was next off the production line, in 1934. Because of similarity many of the parts work on machining for both locos may have been undertaken at the same time.

The photograph below shows 'Flying Scotsman' when it was just completed.

''Flying Scotsman' with a train of original cars.
New 'Garden seat' cars sit on the turntable access line.

Steaming along the garden cutting under the 'rustic' bridge.
Are Randolph and his wife watching?

No 5: **London Midland & Scottish Railway 4-6-0 'Royal Scot'**

Built at Kenton in 1935 from the design and parts obtained from Bassett-Lowke. Because of the Kenton preference for slide vales it has a curved expansion link which is over scale in proportion and also long eccentric rods. This was a willing workhorse and was regularly used on the railway. With Walschaerts valve gear vital proportions are altered when outside admission valves are used instead of inside admission (piston type) valves of the prototype. It is not just a matter of moving everything round 180 degees and, if a correct setting is not prepared at the outset, no amount of cutting and carving will put matters right.

This photograph is taken from a colour glass transparency of the 'Royal Scot'. Randolph was a keen experimenter in early colour photography and this may be one of his. Although the KMR early tradition was to number locomotives with the year in which they were completed the Scot is numbered 935. It is interesting to note that all the KMR photos show the driver sitting inside the

26

tender. It is understood that the tenders were modified to give the driver foot-room but this reduced the coal carrying capacity. Today the current practice is to add foot-rests outside the tender and for the driver to sit on the tender or a driving trolley.

When the railway closed this engine went with Nos 3, 4, 6, and 7 to Cleethorpes but it was not used and simply put into store. Two years later it was purchased by Raymond Marks and, it is thought, it went into store again. It eventually followed No 2 'George V' to the Spinney private railway. It was purchased in 1992/3 by George Clarke and extensively re-built. It took part in the Henry Greenly Rally, held at the Ascot Locomotive Society track in 1994, when I had the great pleasure of driving it on the long and exacting track. It ran superbly. A great credit to its owner and the original builders almost 60 years earlier.

After many years of success at the KMR the 'Royal Scot' found it's way to the Spinney where it is seen pulling a fine set of three coaches. These were scratch built by George Marks along with a fourth which is a dining car.

Driver Geoff Asplin

In 2008 the loco was once again back at the Spinney Light Railway – jointly owned by SLR member Hugh Grant and Alan Ainslie. The SLR has some steep gradients and the 'Royal Scot' still hauls passengers up in style. The SLR owner Alan Ainslie invited members of the Wimborne & District SME to visit his railway In 2007 and I had a second chance to drive the Scot. We had a great time and since then I have had other opportunities to drive this remarkable engine at the Spinney.

No 6: **American 4-8-4 'Northern' with 12 wheeled tender**

[This locomotive seems to have been called a 'Mountain Class'. A 'Mountain' is in fact a 4-8-2. The wheel arrangement of 4-8-4 is a' Northern' or 'Confederation', names which are very rarely used]

Greenly refers to this loco in his second 'ME' article 'Kenton Miniature Railway Re-visited' published in the 16th March 1939 magazine. The engine was designed with Baker valve gear and had 8½"dia driving wheels. The cylinders were 3" bore x 3½" stroke, and Baker's gear was tried on this for the first time and, if successful, it would be used for the planned 4-6-4 'Hudson' which was to follow. The problems with Baker gear were well known at the time but for a slide valve engine it helped to keep the valve travel down. The gear was designed so that all the pins were, as far as possible, balanced. Cantilevering cannot be eliminated in this gear.

With the outbreak of war this was the last locomotive built in the KMR Works until after hostilities ended.

When the KMR railway closed this initially went with the 'NYC Pacific', the 'Flying Scotsman' Pacific the American 4-6-4 'Hudson', and the 'Royal Scot' to Cleethorpes. The long wheelbase prevented it being used at Cleethorpes so it was simply left on display. It's six wheel tender was used by the 'Hudson' - which never had one built for it. From the recent evidence it appears the tender bogies were changed and the original six-wheel tender bogies went along with the engine to an owner in North London who put it into store. Then in 1956 the Goodrington Miniature Railway, Devon, purchased it. One of these owners must have built the new tender.

It is assumed that this new tender was built with access to the original drawings because this loco, now in British Columbia, has a tender virtually the same as the original still with the 'Hudson'. The original tender six wheel bogies had bronze side frames and they

The 'Northern' under construction in 1939

proved too weak for the rugged commercial running of the 'Hudson' at Cleethorpes. Quickly two four wheel bogies, like the ones on the KMR carriages, were fitted. The 'Northern' in Canada still runs on six wheel bronze framed bogies - could they be the original ones?

In the 1960s Walter Kent of Vancouver obtained the loco. He is reported as saying the model which was obtained via the United States. Walter owned Modern Engineering, a machine shop from which he sold model engineering supplies and the odd loco. The engine was not in great shape being well worn. In the 1970s Colin Ming, a member of the British Columbia Society of Model Engineers (BCSME) purchased the 'Northern'. Colin and Brian Shadwick started a thorough overhaul and in June 1979 the BCSME bought the loco and completed the rebuilding. A number of modifications were made during this process. A long sand dome was added and a new poppet valve regulator fitted in the smokebox. This replaced the 'over-scale' needle valve regulator on the backhead. New stainless steel superheaters were made and scale-sized boiler check valves fitted. Two new 6 pint-per-minute injectors were provided. A new steam turret was fitted to the boiler with smaller steam valves. The driving wheels had new steel tyres and re-gauged to 7½"

A Canadian National Railways nameplate and headlight was added, typical of CNR, to the smokebox door. The number 3601 was applied because the new owners believed it was built in 1936 - it is possible the loco was started in this year because No 5 'Royal Scot' was finished in 1935 but, as recorded above, the 'Northern' was completed in 1939. The model was changed to propane firing when it was purchased by the BCSME.

Recently completed, the 'Northern' on the KMR 1939

29

This fine loco is the mainstay of the BCSME's steam locos on their Burnaby (Heritage) Village Museum Railway. It still has the Baker valve gear and, after over 60 years of service, the original copper boiler. As mentioned above the tender retains 12 wheels. The driving wheel flanges were wearing rather thin (Oct 2005) and there were plans to replace them during the coming winter.

The loco consistently pulls 30 passengers up the railway's 1 in 40 gradients. BCSME member Joe Carroll remarks *'Regarded by all as a workhorse of an engine that is forgiving, docile, easy steaming but super powerful to drive. It is a much-loved major loco in our fleet and plays a big part in moving the 30,000 passengers we carry every year between Easter and Thanksgiving.'*

Joe Carroll drives the 'Northern' on the Burnaby track.

NOTE: *In my contacts with Brian Shadwick during 2007 he provided tales of his time in Canada with the BCSME. Much to Brian's pleasure I was able to add his name to this history. Brian lived in Bodmin and I know many railway enthusiasts will treasure, as I do, one of his miniature engineer's oil cans. Sadly Brian passed away just before Christmas 2007.*

No 7: **American 'Hudson' 4-6-4**

Already designed in 1939, and with many of the parts in store, N° 7 had to wait for eight years until after the war. It was not until Jack Newbutt became KMR Works manager in 1947 that he completed this loco, which then had only two years on the railway. This locomotive was a development of N° 6 with larger 10" driving wheels.

The 'Hudson' No.1947 having just been pulled out of the workshops and onto the raised track leading to the turntable. The loco looks very new.

Taken from a glass slide: The unpainted and probably just completed loco with the tender from the 'Northern'. *[The wooden hut, far right, belonged to Harrow & Wembley SME for when club members used their raised track]*

This loco retains the original 'Northern' tender to this day although the six wheeled bogies were replaced with a more rugged four wheel version.

History of the Kenton Miniature Railway

CHAPTER 5

KMR LOCOMOTIVES - WONDERLAND LAKESIDE RAILWAY

When Randolph Jeffress left Kenton Grange in 1949/50 his garden railway was disbanded and five of the locomotives were sold to a miniature railway called the Lakeside Miniature Railway in Cleethorpes. Over a period of years two of them were sold on and the history of the remaining three became linked. These three, although not remaining together for the whole period, spent many years sharing their workload until 2012. In this part of the history we take a nostalgic look at the 1950/60s and the part played by the people who ran the engines.

The three locomotives N°3 'New York Central'; N°4 LNER 'Flying Scotsman' and N°7 'Hudson' 4-6-4 were together for most their working lives from their construction until 2012. This was initially due to Mr Jack Newbutt and later Major John Hext. Jack's involvement with the KMR started after the second World War when he became, on a part-time basis, the fourth and final works manager at Kenton.

He worked at the LNER Neasden Locomotive Depot and, around 1945, he started helping out in the Kenton Grange works. Jack had to move out of his lodgings to make way for a member of the owner's family so he rented, from Mr Jeffress, the former lodge house of the Grange, 'London Lodge', which fronted the Kenton Road.

In 1947 Jack built N°7 using parts already available and the original H Greenly designs. After the closure of the KMR in 1949 the locomotives were sold and five, N°s 3, 4, 5, 6 and 7, went to the miniature railway at Wonderland on the promenade at Cleethorpes. Jack Newbutt gave up his job at Neasden to go north with them. No 5 LMS 'Royal Scot' went into store but N°s 3, 4 and 7 saw active duty on the Lakeside Railway. The long wheelbase of No 6 'Northern' prevented it being used so it was left on display later to be sold.

Jack's son Michael, to be joined later by Rob Foxon in 1957, were both young members of the Lakeside Miniature Railway and they have kindly provided stories of their memories. This part of the history has taken much from their records. Before moving on it is interesting to review the facilities at Wonderland when Jack took his family to Cleethorpes.

On a compact site the structure dominating the whole was the big dipper. 'New Dips' as it was known was constructed in 1921 of Canadian pine. Occupying the area within the dips was the boating lake with its motor boats. Previously there had also been a water chute. Around the boating lake and threading through the dips was the Lakeside Miniature Railway, opened in 1949 with its circular running line. Access to the boating lake was via a walkway which led under the dips and over the miniature railway track on a gated level crossing. Next to the station was a magnificent set of three horse gallopers complete with Gavioli fairground organ which played rousing music all day. Finally, there was the newly installed Peter Pan Railway for the little ones with its sharp turns and much bell ringing by excited youngsters! The whole area was packed with happy holidaymakers determined to have a good time. Interrupting the sound of the fairground organ was the groaning noise of the giant electric motor in the powerhouse adjacent to the miniature railway station, as it hauled the big dipper cars to the highest point on the ride. The light tapping noise heard was the safety device to prevent runaways in case the car stalled or the rope failed. This was soon followed by screams from the riders as the cars descended the deepest dip at speeds in excess of 40mph! There was the pop-pop sound from the motor boats, the crashing of the speedway cars, bell ringing from the Peter Pan railway and of course the sight and smell of real steam on the miniature railway. All this made for an unforgettable experience that was repeated day after day during the summer season, but this was only the outdoor area of Wonderland at the end of the North Promenade. The main part was indoors with dodgems; ghost train; cycledrome; jets; crazy house; side stalls and much more. Wonderland was said to be the largest covered amusement park on the east coast.

When Jack Newbutt arrived in the Autumn of 1949 the Lakeside Miniature Railway had recently been set up by Mr Woolley and ran round the boating lake, probably a distance of ¼ mile. The construction was not very substantial and the track and solitary locomotive not capable of coping with the heavy usage just beginning to happen. This demand was caused by the large numbers of holiday-makers using Cleethorpes for their seaside holiday.

After all the constraints of the post war years this period saw an enormous rise in railway excursions into the town. 'Day trippers' and the 'Factory shut down week' holiday makers came from the industrial towns of Yorkshire. Cleethorpes BR station is on the promenade and ideally placed to deliver passengers into Wonderland. Jack Newbutt was employed to take over the improvement and running of the miniature railway and also to be the engineer to much of the Wonderland amusements.

The loco that had been used to run the railway was a fine scale Bassett-Lowke 'Royal Scot' which was not substantial enough to cope with everyday running but it was kept for display. As Jack arrived during the shut-down period it helped him to get to grips with the task. It was decided to use three of the ex-KMR locomotives and to sell the other two. The three locos were the A1 'Flying Scotsman', the NYC pacific and the 'Hudson'. The 'Northern' 4-8-4 after being on display for the first year, was sold on. The Kenton 'Royal Scot' was not in good condition and had a narrow firebox. It would have made the ten hour daily operation, with the variably coal available, very difficult. It too was sold.

The railway was largely rebuilt. Jack had help from Doug Best who, during the season ran the photography department. The first season was difficult and highlighted the difference between opening a garden railway once a week for pleasure (at Kenton) compared to running seven days a week for profit. Wear and tear on rolling stock resulted in wheels, bearings and all parts that moved were in need of attention even before the end of the season. Fine sand blown from the beach also added to the wear of all moving parts and the track.

'Henrietta' about to start another circuit at the Lakeside Railway

The mainstay of motive power was the 'Hudson' (named 'Henrietta' after Jack's wife) since it was the easiest to keep going for the driver. It was also the most powerful and could handle the biggest trains. The two 'Pacifics' were kept available and used during the quieter week days.

After the second season the railway ran very reliably. Jack and Doug had to work hard out of season to repair and improve all aspects of the railway and maintain the other Wonderland amusements. 'Henrietta' was doing the lion's share of the work on the railway and the improvements to strengthen the motion components really helped. It also showed how inadequate the two other former Kenton locos were for this sort of usage. Of the two 'Pacifics' the American NYC outline one was the lightest build and was little used so, in 1953, it was sold to a Major Hext who was building a private railway on his estate in Coniston, Cumbria. Doug and Jack overhauled and converted the loco to look similar to a BR Clan class for the Major and delivered it to the Coniston Railway. This was the start of further purchases which eventually brought together three of the ex-KMR locomotives. It was also the beginning of Jack and Michael Newbutt's continuing links with the three and their time providing maintenance for the Coniston Railway.

For a time the LNER A1 'Pacific' ran under the guise of an A4 when it was fitted with a chromed streamlined steel shell.

Young Michael driving the disguised 'Flying Scotsman'

At this busy time in 1953 the workshop, situated within the miniature railway, was pushed to the limits. It was decided 'Henrietta'' needed a brother so a start was made on building a new steam locomotive. This was to be a workhorse designed to be easily maintained and driver friendly as well as easy on the track. While the new loco was under construction in 1954 Major Hext purchased the A1 'Flying Scotsman' so extra work was created by the preparation and delivery to Cumbria.

The new engine was completed in 1955 and this 4-4-4 loco 'Grimsby Town' (named after the local football club) was revealed. Not very pretty and not based on any prototype the new engine was a great success. Indeed it continued running the railway alone under Doug Best's management when Jack had moved on and the other locos had been sold in 1959.

"Grimsby Town" ready to give "Henrietta" a hand with the holidaymakers.

At the age of nine in 1957 Rob Foxon joined as a junior. The railway was being worked by 'Grimsby Town' and 'Henrietta' with two complete trains of six articulated carriages (seating 24 passengers each). There were also a couple of additional articulated pairs (seating 8 passengers each) which could be added to lengthen either train at busy times. With one set added there was capacity for 32 passengers per train. This could be an everyday requirement, so it can be appreciated why the other smaller locos could not cope! It was at that time that Rob overheard conversations about a miniature railway at Coniston in the Lake District, although as a youngster, he neither appreciated where this was, or that Jack Newbutt was involved in its development. He does remember however, a strange locomotive being worked on in the Wonderland workshops at that time, which he believes may have been the NYC, newly named 'Holywath' for the Major, receiving attention

Rob spent six gloriously happy summer seasons from 1957 to 1962 working on the miniature railway at weekends and during school holidays at first under Jack Newbutt and later, Doug Best.

A day on the railway would start at about 10.00am with the lighting of the fire from cold. When the fire had been established, a compressor driven blower helped to speed up the process. The full working boiler pressure of 'Grimsby Town' was 125psi ('Henrietta' 100psi). When about 60psi had been reached, steaming could be completed without further assistance. Everything was ready for the first passengers by about 11.30am. Busiest times were early afternoons onwards with trains often filled to capacity. The ride was two circuits of the main line and cost 6d (2½p), the train running non-stop through the station and over the level crossing for the second circuit. Rob literally did anything required at any time but his regular daily duties on running days were ticket collecting and level crossing gateman. The crossing had only one gate and it was often challenging to hold people back from the un-gated side of the track for the little train to pass! Rob was not old enough to become a regular driver but learned a lot about steam locomotive practice and was often entrusted to put the engine away at night. Highlights during this time were several particularly busy Sunday's when two trains were operated by using the loop.

Schoolboy friends driving: Ray Crome 'Grimsby Town' and Michael Newbutt 'Henrietta'

It was his job on days like this to act as signalman working the electrically operated point on the seaward side of the railway to switch the trains into the loop after their first circuit of the main line. He remembers on one occasion, some rowdy youths were energetically rocking the carriages as the train passed over the crossing at speed. A few moments later as it rounded the bridge over the lake, the train tipped over completely. All he could see from the crossing was the underside of the carriages and the de-railed tender of

'Grimsby Town'. Fortunately, apart from a thoroughly deserved wetting, there were no injuries but the incident did warrant a mention in local news.

Rob would call in at the workshop occasionally during the winter closed season to keep in touch. The track inside the workshop building was dual gauge to accommodate both seven and a quarter and ten and a quarter inch rolling stock. Outside contract work was sometimes undertaken. The equipment (lathe, milling machine, etc) were belt driven from a series of line shafts and pulleys by a large electric motor situated in a corner of the workshop. Health & Safety would take a very dim view of this practice today! One of his jobs was to start the motor up when required. He remembers the lights dimming during the run up process! The noise of the line shafts in operation could be heard from some distance outside the shop when machines were being used. Winter maintenance of the loco's involved the removal of the boiler for annual inspection, together with any other work found to be required. This was made easier by having a section of track mounted on a trestle stand, thus enabling work to be undertaken at waist level. Settling almost one ton of locomotive on this and its subsequent removal was a hair raising process involving the use of an eight foot length of rail held in mid air from the stand down to terra firma, supported in several places by anything that came to hand; together with several burley helpers to push!

In 1959 Jack Newbutt left Wonderland for employment in Amersham, Bucks. It is thought he could see the writing on the wall for seaside resorts like Cleethorpes. At the age of 44 he probably wanted a more secure future. Shortly after this 'Henrietta' was dismantled because of boiler problems and did not run again until she was rebuilt in 1975 by Jack and Michael which leads on to the story of the three locos at Coniston.

History of Kenton Miniature Railway

CHAPTER 6

THREE LOCOMOTIVES - CONISTON RAILWAY

Subsequently, one by one over a period of 24 years, the three locos were purchased by Major Hext the owner of the garden railway on the lower slopes of the Old Man of Coniston.

A special method for re-numbering the locos was adopted for the Cumbria garden railway: the first digit is the acquisition sequence, and the next two give the year acquired. Hence Kenton's N° 3, the first loco purchased in 1954, became N°154 and was named 'Holywath'. The LNER 'Pacific' became N°255 'Trenarren'.

Meanwhile N°7 'Henrietta' left Cleethorpes and in 1974 Jack Newbutt heard it was in pieces in Littlehampton. Jack and Michael agreed to assemble her and also to refurbish 'Grimsby Town' which was destined to join her. Before taking 'Henrietta' back to Littlehampton it was agreed she would go to Coniston for trials where Major Hext was very impressed and agreed to retain the original name.

Michael Newbutt with 'Henrietta' on trials at the Coniston Railway after her rebuilding

Jack Newbutt with 'Grimsby Town' at Littlehampton after the locos' overhaul

The Coniston Railway had a zig-zag joining two main levels. The linking track ran through a cutting and tunnel, which was officially no less

41

than 1:15 at its steepest point. Michael Newbutt thinks a survey showed that in part of the tunnel a staggering 1:12 existed. All the trains needed a banker to make the climb.

The boiler of 'Trenarren' (Flying Scotsman) was used to replace the similar one in 'Holywath' which was damaged when it boiled dry. This led to a modification to the A1. To ensure maximum power on this demanding railway the cylinders were bored out as far as they would go. The stroke was lengthened and the driving wheel diameter reduced. The final step was to increase boiler pressure with a larger firebox with greater heating surface and more steam space. This was achieved by fitting a belpaire type boiler. The appearance was spoilt but the loco was then powerful enough to cope with the steep inclines.

Ex-KMR 'Flying Scotsman' as 'Trenarren' [stands woth 'Henrietta' at Signal box.

Photo: David Robinson

'Trenarren' backs gently down the 1/15 gradient with the banker adding safety breaking power.

Photo: David Robinson

42

To cope with the 1 in 15 incline 'Henrietta' was fitted with a tender booster. The additional tender drive, via a two cylinder steam engine, is engaged by a dog-clutch. This drives the leading axel of the front bogie through a reduction gear. The second axel is driven by an outside chain drive. Power is transmitted to the second bogie by an ex-Mini constant velocity drive shaft. Both axels of the second bogie are driven in the same way as the front with an outside chain. The second bogie had an air brake system which works on all four wheels. Although the loco could take the incline it always used the banker in the interests of safety.

'Henrietta' ready for an open day at the Coniston Railway   David Robinson

The American locos [ex KMR NYC Pacific] was modified to look more like BR Clan class but it's origins could still be traced. As recorded above Jack had, in 1959, moved back to Amersham but he, his son Michael and grandson, continued to travel to the Lake District to run and service the three locos at Coniston. After Jack's death in 2005 Michael continued to maintain the Coniston locos.

'NYC 1933' Pacific as 'Holywath' at Coniston   D Robinson

43

One of the triple articulated passenger sets from the KMR was at Coniston, maintained in running order. The track contained some sections of Kenton rails and even some from the British Empire Exhibition of 1924.

The story of the three locos came to an end in 2012. Major Hext died in 2009 and the Coniston Railway was destined to be dismantled. It was hoped the railway would be sold with the house and land but, like the end of the KMR in 1949, it was not to be. On the 26th May 2012 Michael C L Hodgson, Auctioneers, conducted the sale of the railway. Three new owners had plans for their acquisitions.

More photos are in the new Album attached to this history.

CHAPTER 7

AFTER CONISTON – CLEETHORPES AGAIN

After the sale of the Coniston Railway stock and equipment the three locomotives were parted. 'Trenarren' went to Ian Page to be refurbished. The other two are virtually still together because Rob Foxon purchased 'Henrietta' and his son Steve successfully bid for 'Holywath'. Rob also obtained an ex-KMR single 'garden seat' passenger car. It is intended to return 'Henrietta', as near as possible, to the condition in which she ran at Wonderland (Michael Newbutt found and passed on the original smoke deflectors). Steve plans to remodel the NYC 1933 'Pacific' to the KMR form.

Initially Rob arranged to display 'Henrietta' in the Cleethorpes Coast Light Railway Museum and produced a press release 'Henrietta comes home'. Four of those originally associated with the Wonderland Lakeside Railway came together to meet the Press. Rob Foxon, Doug Best, Ray Crome and Michael Newbutt celebrated the return of the locomotive to Cleethorpes.

'Henrietta' arrives in the Cleethorpes Coast Light Railway Museum

Michael Newbutt and his schoolboy friend Ray Crome have remained life-long friends. Ray had been an apprentice at Immingham shed and Doncaster Railway Works to become a qualified engineer. Efforts to achieve the planned future of the locomotives had moved along. 'Henrietta' was in Ray's workshop stripped down and well on her way to being in near Kenton look. It is intended she will look the same as when running at Wonderland which only had a few minor changes to the original when built at the KMR.

'Holywath' remained in it's ex Coniston Railway condition and has replaced 'Henrietta' on display at the Cleethorpes museum along with the single 'garden seat' coach.

The Foxons purchased track from Coniston with the intention of using half for a demonstration line at Cleethorpes and half for a similar set up at the Leicester Museum of Technology, Abbey Pumping Station. The Cleethorpes Coast Light Railway is an extensive 15 inch gauge line along the coast. As such 'Henrietta' is unable to use the track, hence the need for a demonstration line in 7¼ inch gauge. Consideration was given to running on the local track run by the Grimsby & Cleethorpes Model Engineering Society but, like most similar societies, there are no storage facilities for owner's locomotives. All locos have to be transported to and from the track on running days which is not suitable for the heavy 'over-scale' loco.

CHAPTER 8

LOCOMOTIVE DRAWINGS

The loco that never was? Discovered in Jack Newbutt's KMR papers was this very battered general arrangement drawing of a Highland Railway 4-4-0 Loco. Drawn by Henry Greenly on 23 April 1938 and given the name 'Kenton' In the bottom right-hand corner Greenly noted 'Rebuild of GER 4-4-0' Was this a project being considered as a 'new' locomotive for the KMR? We know Randolph Jeffress was keen to have models of american style engines and the first, the NYC Pacific, was built in 1933. However, British outlines followed in 1934 and 1935 then there was a four year gap to the 'Northern' 4-8-4 in 1939. So this idea may have been a stop-gap just to provide a new model. We will probably never know as it was apparently never taken any further.

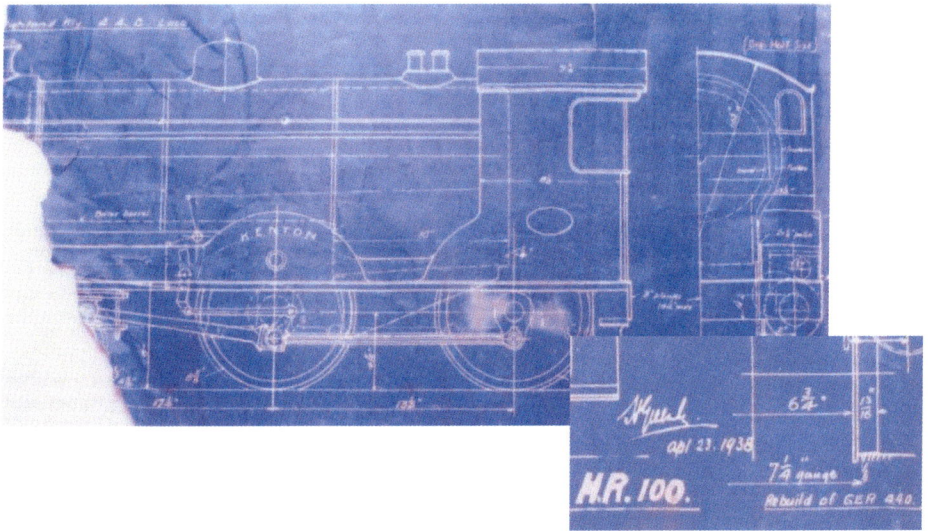

Detail from the bottom corner of the drawing numbered HR.100.   Signed 'H Greenly Apl 23.1938'

Drawing of the American "Pacfic" NYC 4-6-2 by Henry Greenly

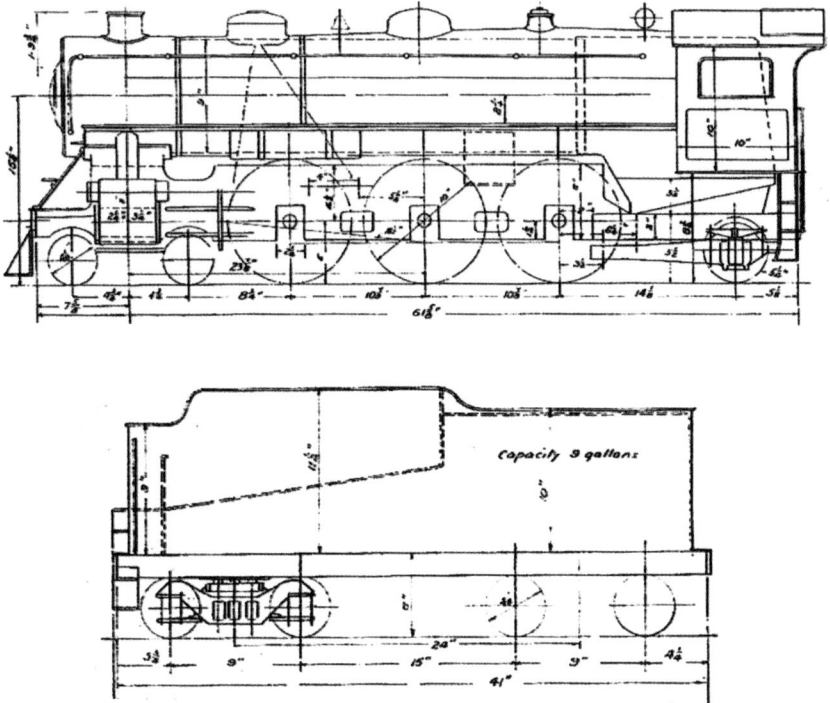

The tender drawing showing details of the American style bogie which are the same as used by the KMR on the passenger cars.

This was the first of the three USA type locomotives and came from the meeting and discussion at the Model Engineer Exhibition when Randolf Jeffress and Henry Greenly first met. The design used many similar parts and castings as the LNER "Flying Scotsman" pacific already under construction in the Kenton workshops at that time.

Previously in this history it was explained the 'Northern' was wrongly called a 'Mountain' class loco. When the loco ended up in the British Columbia Society of Model Engineers they numbered it 1936 because it was thought to have been built in that year. In fact the loco was not built until 1939 (someone suggested turning the 6 upside down to correct the error). It retains the earlier date to this day. Where did these mistakes originate? A number of original Greenly drawings exist and the date on the tender and cab side may explain. The heading 'Mountain type' the other.

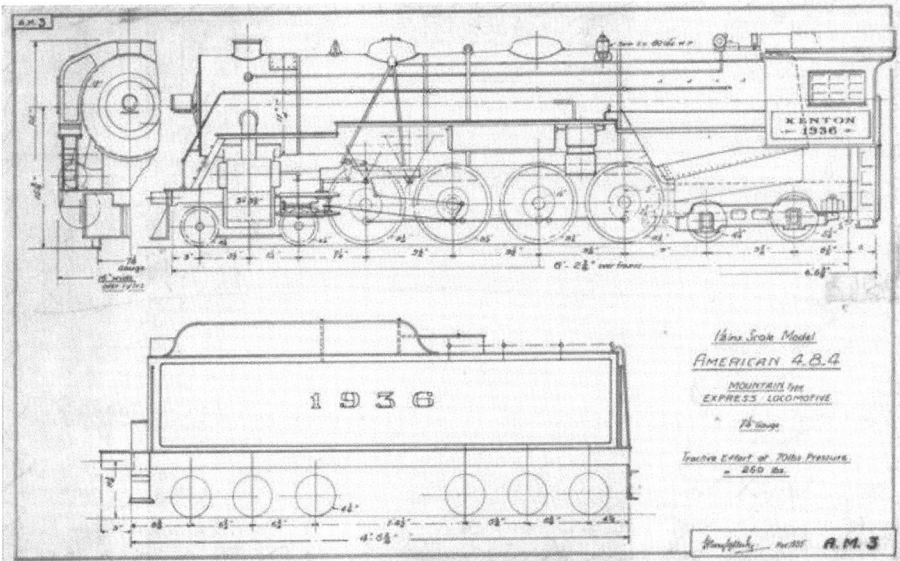

Out of focus title reads:

1½ins Scale Model
AMERICAN 4-8-4
MOUNTAIN Type
EXPRESS LOCOMOTIVE
7¼" Gauge
Tractive Effort at 70lbs Pressure
- 260 lbs

Henry Greenly May 1935 **A.M.3**

Drawing of the Hudson type (4-6-4) by Henry Greenly

This was similar to the "Northern" (4-8-4) locomotive built in 1939. It was intended to use the same 12 wheel tender design designed for the earlier model. The parts and castings were kept in store during the WW2 years and in 1949 Jack Newbutt built the loco. A tender for this loco was not built and the "Northern's" tender was transferred to the new loco. Somewhere along the line a new 12 wheel tender was built for the "Northern" probably while the loco was at the Goodrington Miniature Railway in Devon.

CHAPTER 9

WHERE ARE THEY NOW?

In January 2015 as I bring my involvement with this history to an end I have collected some information from the current owners of the locomotives. I wanted to find out what the future lies for each of them and to see if a recent photograph or two can be included. Right away with No 1 I have to admit there is little to report and no updated photograph.

No 1   Great Central Railway 4-6-0 'Immingham' Class

As far as I can establish Immingham is still with Christopher Finken's Railway and is still going strong. It is remarkable that after 107 years the loco still exists. Like all seven it bears testament to the dedicated maintenance spent on them over the years and the strength of their original design and constructors. Mainly thanks to Henry Greenly, Bassett-Lowke and the KMR workshop team.

No 2   London & North Western Railway 4-4-0 'George the Fifth'

This loco is still owned by Hugh Ballentyne-Dykes and is kept at the Spinney Light Railway in Surrey. It has a current boiler certificate and runs occasionally on open days at the railway. (More on update below see Royal Scot.)

No 3   NYC 1933 American 'Pacific' 4-6-2 (small New York Central type)

Still in it's guise as a BR Clan Class from Coniston Railway days it is on display at the Cleethorpes Coast Light Railway Museum along with an ex-KMR 'garden seat' coach. Owned by Steven Foxon who hopes it can be restored to it's original KMR condition. Steven hopes to run the engine at the University of Leicester Museum of Technology at the Abbey Pumping Station where half the ex-Coniston track could be installed as a demonstration line.

When work on his father's loco 'Henrietta' [see page 55] is complete it is planned to carry out a complete assessment to see how feasible it is to return the loco back to the Kenton 'NYC 1933' condition with 'KMR' on the tender.

No 4   LNER 'Pacific' 4-6-2 'Flying Scotsman'

Purchased at the Coniston sale by Ian Page who, it was thought at the time, planned to restore it as an original LNER 'Flying Scotsman' with a new boiler.

No 5   LMS 4-6-0 'Royal Scot'

The 'Royal Scot' 6109 'Royal Engineer' is still at the Spinney Light Railway and is in shared ownership of one of the railway's volunteers, David Grant, and the owner of the SLR, Alan Ainslie.   The loco has a current boiler certificate and usually runs on open days.

On the 14th June 2014 I visited the SLR when the 'George V' 4-4-0 and the Scot were both in steam. The owner of 'George V', Hugh Ballentyne-Dykes, kindly let me drive it, much to my delight. After a shower of rain the loco was light footed on this demanding railway but I enjoyed the challenge.

I renewed my contact by having another drive of the Scot which again proved to be a powerful loco. There are no plans for these two engines which will remain for the foreseeable future at the Spinney.

Above: Alan Ainslie with the Royal Scot and Hugh Ballentyne-Dykes with George V.
Right: Author and Hugh

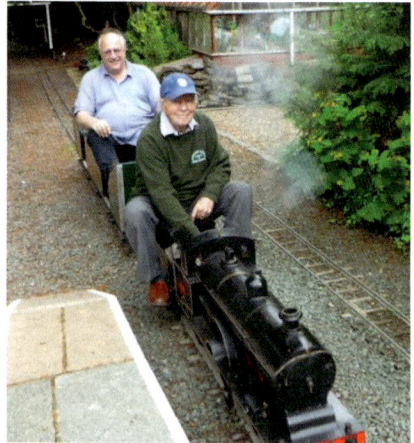

During my visit I talked with Hugh about his father Joe the original owner of the Spinney Railway. He explained another coincidence in this history. His father lived in Cumbria during his early years and acquired his interest in railways by spending time in the local signal box. He was school friends with John Hext and the Major's Coniston Railway was the inspiration which led to the building of the Spinney Light Railway in 1974. The fact that there were ex-KMR locos at Coniston may have been the spur for Joe to seek out and acquire two of them for his railway.

No 6   No 1939 American 4-8-4 with 12 wheel tender 'Northern'

Once "missing" locomotive the 'Northern' is now in British Columbia, Canada. Owned by the British Columbia Society of Model Engineers it has been in the wars recently and as present is undergoing a major refurbishment. Boiler troubles were resolved in 2012 when, thanks to the engineering skills of the team, the original was repaired and despite modern standards passed certification with flying colours.

In 2014 the loco was taken out of service due to noisy running gear. Alan Pointing, a new member, offered to make new bushes but when the wheels were removed the crank pins were found to be badly worn. The worn out axel box bushes confirmed heavy use over the years. New axels and crank pins were necessary.

At least two of the original spoked wheels had cracks. These had been welded when the wheels were re-tyred in the past but two had failed again. It was decided to have new BoxPok wheels designed and machined using 4140 chrome moly steel. These have been delivered and have been black powder coated. A couple of new connecting rods have been machined to replace those that were distorted.

Other parts requiring attention: Spring hangers; Valve gear bushings and pins; Crankpins; Rear truck axel bearings; Rear truck wheels and the rebuilding the reversing links.

The major repairs have been completed but some of the minor ones will be left until after the current running season. From the very long list of problems it can be appreciated this really is a major rebuild. The loco is one of the mainstays of the British Columbia Society's on their track in Burnaby and the expense and effort is worthwhile.

Original wheel: cracks and repairs

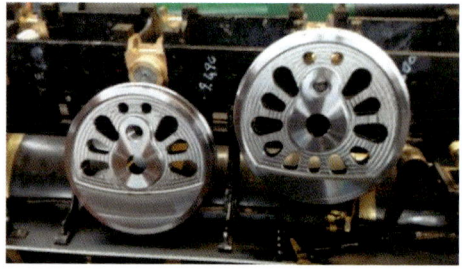
The new Boxpok driving wheels and axe bearings

Having repaired the boiler the running gear required attention. New member Alan Ponting takes his first survey of the 'Northern' set up on the Club's workshop "rotisserie"

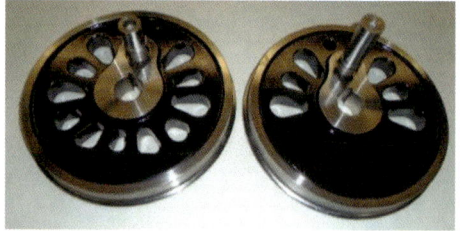

Powder coated BoxPox wheels and new crank pins

The wheels back on and getting closer to completing the first phase of the overhaul

No 7   No 1947 American 4-6-4 Express Locomotive 'Hudson'

In the workshop of Ray Crome the work to restore the 'Henrietta" to Wonderland condition is almost complete. Owned by Rob Foxon it is intended to run on a demonstration track built from half the ex-Coniston track. This will be installed alongside a stretch of the 10¼ inch gauge Cleethorpes Coast Light Railway close to the site of the dismantled Wonderland.

Left: Henrietta is restored to her Wonderland livery.

Right: The loco under her final steam test.

Finally the tender needs some attention. The power bogies installed by Jack Newbutt for the severe incline at Coniston are to be removed and the original bogies replaced.

History of the Kenton Miniature Railway

CHAPTER 10

HARROW'S LOST RAILWAY

After the War Mrs Stella Jeffress, was residing in a retirement home. Mr Randolph Jeffress was looking after the family home Kenton Grange with his wife and son. The KMR started operating again but the 'wild' areas of garden had not recovered from the neglect accrued during the war years. The wooden station building disappeared leaving a simple cross-over without platforms for the passengers. At sometime Randolph divorced his American wife and apparently around 1948 married his housekeeper Constance. In the late 1940s two events resulted in the closure of the railway. Firstly, Randolph's mother Mrs Stella Jeffress decided she wished to return to the Grange. This reportedly caused a certain amount of friction and Randolph decided he must leave the family home. Secondly, the cost of maintaining the property had become too much to bear and negotiations were started with Wembley Borough Council [now Brent Council] to see if they would buy the Grange.

Extracts from Council Minutes show that Randolph had hoped to keep the KMR running and to occupy London Lodge (now demolished), on Kenton Road. The Council had no objection to the continuation of the railway but would not agree to his living anywhere on the estate. The railway was disbanded and Randolph moved to the Edgware area. It was finally agreed that the Council would purchase a 21 year lease for £12,500 and the lease was signed in the middle of 1952. Shortly after the Wembley Council in turn leased the manor house to the Middlesex County Council who converted it, and the immediate grounds into an elderly people's home. The main area of the grounds was used to build a small estate of houses and bungalows for pensioners. The remainder was incorporated into Woodcock Hill Park. The workshops and stable block were used, as they are to-day, for homes and a store for the park grounds-man's equipment.

When the family moved out of the Grange Mrs Stella Jeffress obtained a house in Northwick Circle, Kenton, where she lived until her death in 1964. In the early 1970s one local writer visited Mrs Constance Jeffress, who was still living at that time in Edgware, to confirm his known facts about the family. Constance died in 1977.

On 3rd August 1967 Randolph died in Harrow aged 67, recorded occupation 'of independent means'. So a famous local pioneering miniature railway passed into history. The railway was built at a time when 'gentlemen with money' were taking up a novel form of garden transport. Some of the stately homes used small gauge railways as an integral part of work on their large estates. The 15"gauge Ravenglass and Eskdale and the Romney Hythe & Dymchurch were the ultimate miniature railways which provided regular local transport services for the public. Henry Greenly's association with many of these projects and his experience with the Kenton Grange Railway were all part of the wider history of the development of miniature railways and model engineering. Although he was not a famous engineer, Randolph Jeffress played a part in that story of successful miniature railways.

We recall that Bassett-Lowke wrote in Model Engineer:

> "Mr Jeffress, of Kenton Grange, who has one of the largest
> collections of 7¼ inch gauge locomotives in the country, finds
> that this fulfils his garden railway requirements on the
> comprehensive line he is laying."

Kenton Miniature Railway: Photo Album
All photographs from the Newbutt Collection unless otherwise noted

'Flying Scotsman' Young Michael Newbutt at the controls of a well-used loco   c 1948

'Northern' in new condition unpainted with its painted tender   c 1939

c1939

'Northern' now painted. Although not a complete photo of the loco it is included because it shows the construction of the turntable. It also demonstrates the quality of the workmanship of the KMR Works. Lasting quality where today it is still passenger hauling on the Burnaby Village Museum Railway, Canada.

'Royal Scot' Randolph Jeffress encouraged children to get involved in the running of his railway and many had a chance to drive. Perhaps none were as young as this one. This photo also shows the loco on the end of the bridge over the pond. The curved side of the pond can be seen in the bottom right corner under the metal bridge support.

c 1946

60

'Hudson' Jack Newbutt constructed this locomotive in 1947 using parts purchased before the WW2. These two photos show the newly built engine.

Top: Unpainted with the borrowed 'Northern' tender.
Bottom: Complete with smoke deflectors and a new coat of paint. Michael snug in the tender.

'Immingham' From his signature goggles on his head this is Randolph who is preparing the loco. The compressed air blower to draw the fire and Randolph's handful of kindling wood shows it is just about to be lit.

The lady looking down (top left of photo) and her son(?) are featured in the second photo below. The boy with his hand under the loco is thought to be Randolph's son Godfrey.

Immingham' steams gently ready for the waiting passengers.

From the lady's hat fashion this could be in the war but the box carried by her son is not apparently large enough to be a gas mask so it may be a camera.

The lad with his sleeves rolled up is possibly Randolph's son Godfrey.

62

'Immingham' A clear shot of the works. This photo also shows the substantial size of the rails in this area near the workshops

'Hudson' Here are the 3 tracks passing near the workshop. Main line on right with the loco standing on a passing loop. Left the service line for steaming up and gaining access to the workshops via the turntable. Driver is Bruce (Newbutt)

Garden cutting. A boy on the rustic bridge watches a train crossing the garden. The train will shortly pass over the pond and pass along the rear of the workshop the roof of which can be seen in the background.

The train has come to a halt and everyone, including the driver, seems to be very interested in something going on in the middle of the garden.

The Tunnel. This photo by C D Bradshaw depicts the NYC Pacific emerging from the tunnel which was constructed from a wooden building with both ends removed. The train is coming out of the hut at the northern 'garden' end. At the southern end it was extended with a mass of foliage.

The Station
Above: a group of children learn about the magic of steam.

Left: The same party pass through the station behind the NYC Pacific.

65

............and so to bed !

The 'Hudson' is pushed into the workshop through the small access door at the end of a busy running day.

'Flying Scotsman' In 1952 with Jack Newbutt at the controls on the Lakeside Railway

'NYC Pacific' A bright sunny morning as fascinated bystanders watch Jack prepare the loco for running.

The three locos at CONISTON

The three ex-KMR locos at Coniston. Left to right: 'NYC Pacific' [Holywath] 4-6-0; 'Hudson' [Henrietta] 4-6-4 and 'Flying Scotsman' [Trenarren] 4-6-0.

'Henrietta' Photographed in 1978 in the first livery after refurbishment for the Coniston Railway

'Henrietta' in her 2007 livery.

Addenda 1

Copy of an article by Henry Greenly for the Model Engineer and Practical Electrician magazine dated 4th January 1934 :

An American "Pacific" Model for 7¼ in. Gauge
By Henry Greenly, A.I.Loco.E.

At one of the recent "ME" Exhibitions Mr J R Jeffress discussed with me the design and construction of a free-lance 1½ in. scale "Pacific" model for his garden railway. He had just finished a model of the L.N.W.R. (L.M.S) "George the Fifth" 4–4–0 type express loco, from the Bassett-Lowke castings, and desired something more powerful for his next machine. The outcome has been the building of the engine illustrated. The diagram of the locomotive included the leading dimensions of the engine, and as far as possible the minor details are the same as the L.N.E.R. "Pacific" which is at the moment "going through the shops" at Mr Jeffress' private residence.

By special request, slide valve cylinders were arranged for. To simplify construction, and to make the valve gear centres interchangeable with my standard double ported piston valve cylinders, the combination lever was attached at the top to a special form of crosshead guide supported from the valve gear girder frames. The drop lug on this guide is attached to the valve spindle by fore-and-aft nuts, this providing for the final setting

Messrs Roberts, Jeffress and Greenly

of the valves under steam, if need be.

Utmost care has been exercised in getting accurate wheel patterns and the bogie, trailing and tender wheels are solid. The balance weights of the coupled wheels are of the applied type, these patterns being intended for either two, three or four cylinder engines.

The boiler is made of copper throughout, with riveted and fullered joints, the final caulking being soft solder of "aircraft" quality. The barrel is 9 in. diameter (solid drawn copper tubing), and the plates are 5/32 in. and 3/16 in. thick. The tubes are 47 in number, and are 5/8 in. outside diameter. My 1903 Undertype regulator is used, and, as readers know, this is a disc valve arranged in a tube in the barrel of the boiler. As designed, it can be easily withdrawn, and steam is taken from the inner dome. The cap of this dome is also easily re-moveable with a large spanner.

The NYC "Pacific nearing completion and showing the boiler before lagging

The firebox is fixed to the frames by the late Mr. H. A. Ivatts' (G.N.R.) pattern of flexible expansion holding down plate. The fire-door is of the G.W.R. sliding type, one lever governing the two doors. Mr Jeffress also suggested a method of making the smokebox so that it can be entirely withdrawn, leaving all the steam pipes intact.

The engine has been finished in Mr. Jeffress' workshop only a few days before going to press with this issue, and, while a preliminary steam test on the track has been made, more or less in the dark, when minor troubles are cleared out of the way, and better weather prevails for garden railway work, I hope I shall be able to say something definite about performances.

Mr. E. H. Roberts has been responsible for nine-tenths of the work, and with Mr. Jeffress and myself is shown alongside his handiwork. Mr. Jeffress has taken every interest in the details of the work during the construction, and also recorded much of it with his excellent home cine camera. We only await the summer for more of his interesting railway pictures.

Addenda 2

[with permission of the Model Engineer]

Copy of an article by Henry Greenly for the Model Engineer magazine dated 16th March 1939 :

Kenton Miniature Railway Re-visited
By Henry Greenly, A.I.Loco.E.

Soon after Mr. J. R. Jeffress's 7¼" gauge garden railway at Kenton Grange, Kenton, near Harrow, Middlesex, was freely opened to visitors and friends some years ago, it was the rule of the road to lay down one "new keel" every season. This was more or less maintained at the outset, but as the engines now being planned are getting more ambitious in size and type, the programme in respect to timetable is, perhaps, a little more difficult to maintain. However, there is no shortage in the motive power department of the line. The varied types running each week make things all the more interesting, and, as will be seen from the notes which follow, there is also certainly no shortage in the work facing the Kenton Miniature Railway workshops in the immediate future.

The model locomotives at present in running condition are enumerated below:-

(1) Great Central Railway 4-6-0 type "Immingham" Class.
(2) L.N.W. Railway (L.M.S.), 4-4-0 type "George V"
(3) L.M.S. Railway, 4-6-0 type "Royal Scot,"
(4) L.N.E. Railway, "Pacific" 4-6-2, "Flying Scotsman,"
(5) The American "Pacific" (small N.Y.C. type).

For the most part these engines have been built or finished off at Kenton, and will soon be supplemented by a new 4-8-4 type large American "Mountain" type passenger engine with a twelve wheel tender. This last metioned locomotive is one of three engines which were planned a couple of years ago, and which will, as far as possible, be interchangeable in details. Only two of the three have proceeded towards any degree of completeness. The second is to be an American 4-6-4 or "Hudson" type express engine with the new "standard" 3"cylinders and 10" diameter coupled wheels.

As Mr. Jeffress's engines, except the American "Pacific" (see "M.E." January 4th, 1934), have not been in any great length described in these pages, it may be mentioned that the Great Central (now L.N.E.) Railway "Immingham" was a model of one of Mr. J. G. Robinson's successful express engines. It was built some thirty years ago for Mr. Ernest Coats (of the well known cotton firm), and was, perhaps. the first really successful passenger-hauling garden railway engine made in this gauge. It was built by Messrs. Bassett-Lowke, of Northampton, and in preparing the drawings the writer interpreted the details of the prototype as faithfully as he knew how. Standards for tyre widths, gauge dimensions, had at this date to be determined, and such figures are still in common usage.

The model has a copper boiler made in the orthodox fashion, a method yet to be recommended by the writer, except where new processes of silver-soldering now available would suggest improvement. The engine still puts up a good performance, and with an average train-load is know to have a remarkably good turn of speed. It is only beaten by the more modern "Royal Scot". Here Campbell's cylinders, machined by the famous E.N.V. people, are fitted.

The valve-gear is Stephenson's link motion arranged with curved expansion-links in an over-scale proportion and long eccentric rods (see illustration Fig.185 of the writer's larger model steam loco. Book, "Model Steam Locomotives" from P. Marshall & Co. Ltd. Post free 6s. 6d.)

The next engine in the list is a London & North Western locomotive of a type still running on the successor system, the L.M.S.R. This is a 1909 model designed and was heralded by Bassett-Lowke as a not-too-expensive 4-4-0 engine for the then becoming popular 7¼" gauge railway. The "George the Vth" batch came out some years later than the original "Precursors" but from a model point of view there were only small differences in design.

This model was the first locomotive completely built at "Kenton Works". At the same time as it was progressing, Messrs. Jackson & Roberts were constructing the American "Pacific" engine, in which as many parts and drawings that could be worked in from the L.N.E.R. "Pacific" model then going through the drawing office were used.

The "Kenton" L.N.E.R. "Pacific" "Flying Scotsman" followed, and the next year Mr. J. R. Jeffress started building a "Royal Scot" for which a model locomotive from the same drawing board was being built by Bassett-Lowke. The advantage, from the point of view of the Kenton railway's management, was that this made a full range of castings readily available.

All K.M. Railway's engines are built with slide valve cylinders and in adapting designs for piston valve prototypes, modifications to valve-gear have to be considered. As most readers are aware, with Walschaerts, vital proportions are altered when outside admission-valves are used instead of the inside admission (piston type) valves of the prototype are employed. It is not just a matter of moving everything around 180 degrees, and if a proper setting out is not prepared at the outset, no amount of cutting and carving, or of such valve setting modifications commonly adopted in dealing with Stephenson's link-motion, will put matters to rights.

In the earlier days of Kenton Railway the track was not of the heaviest type. Hence the design of the first American was modified to suit the wheel loads common to the English models then existent or building. The "post and beam" type of support was in being over a considerable length of the line, and while derailments were few, they were always feared. Where children are among the passengers on a narrow track they often act thoughtlessly, and care in all constructional details is essential. On all parts of the track where levels have to be above the normal surface of the ground, embankments have been reared up and the track is now almost entirely supported on *terra firma,* Such ballast material as could be obtained being concentrated under the sleepers. The difficulty about all "post and beam" model permanent ways is that climatic conditions cause the beams to twist in every direction, even if they have sufficient strength to carry the load. It will be remembered that Mr. Isambard K. Brunel's system of piles and longitudinals laid down just one hundred years ago for the G.W. Railway, was abandoned before the line progressed beyond Maidenhead. The beam (i.e the longitudinal sleeper) certainly saw the broad gauge through to the end, but it did not make a good road. As soon as the gauge was altered, economic considerations as well as the others, led to the standardisation of the cross sleeper.

The new track at Kenton is laid with 9 lb. per yard commercial flat-bottom rails, tied with pressed corrugated steel sleepers intermingled with creosoted wooden sleepers. The wooden sleepers were available at the conversion of the track, and, of course, were used up. This rail makes a most satisfactory garden railway track. The rail is heavy enough to keep the line in a "stayed-put" condition, with the least amount of track maintenance work. The important fact about model railway laying out-of-doors is that failing the use of highly expensive graded angular ballast, perfectly supported on a drained sub-foundation, a large number of sleepers of sufficiently robust a character to stand weather conditions, suitable fastenings, and a scale loading, it is better to use a heavy rail and sleepers, which are possibly both quite out of scale. A 1½" scale sleeper would measure in cross-section 1¼" x 5/8", and a scale rail would work out at about 1½ lb. per yard run. A scale railway carriage would only have a loading of about 30 lb. per axel. On the Kenton line, with two adult passengers per truck, the loading per axel often exceeds 100 lb. Actually, a 4" x 2" section sleeper is about the limit that can be recommended, but a 5½" x 2½" timber provides really a desirable size to withstand the rigours of our climate and gives a suitable base for a 9 lb. rail. The use of this rail which is about the smallest commercially rolled section that is economical, will last many years in the open air, and, with steel sleepers, is not difficult to lay. These pressed sections can be obtained properly punched for suitable rail fastenings, and thus maintain the correct gauge even if for other reasons they are supplemented by creosoted wood sleepers.

Another outstanding feature of the Kenton permanent way is the use of the cast frogs for the points and crossings. These are used throughout and are supplemented by pivoted points. The point rails were formed out of standard M.S. flats. The section used is 2" x ½" or 3/8", and to prevent the section overturning, the two point rails are bolted together, as show in the detail herewith. This scheme saves a lot of work forming a flat-bottomed rail into a point blade, and is well worthy of emulation. Mr. Jeffress and his works' staff are to be congratulated on the idea. Slide chairs are not necessary; a piece of flat plate suffices for the point rails to move upon.

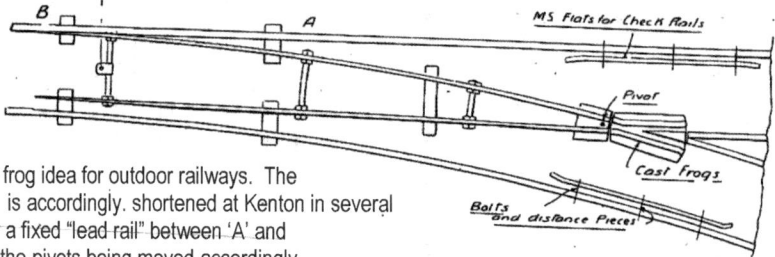

The cast frog idea for outdoor railways. The point rail is accordingly. shortened at Kenton in several cases by a fixed "lead rail" between 'A' and the frog, the pivots being moved accordingly.

Locomotive building having occupied most of the activities of the Kenton works for some time, nothing further of note can be recorded, except a continuance of the making of bogie trucks for all ages of passengers. The standard bogies are used, some of them as supports for articulated trucks. To allow ample room for both children and adults alike, the body dimensions have been increased in width and length. The buffers are simply adequate blocks of wood, so that buffer locking troubles are non-existent.

From details on the drawings for the engines under construction it is possible to modify the original design as it develops. Then, when the engine is finished, final general arrangements can be made which can serve for both 3½" (3/4" scale) as well as the 1½" scale machines. However, nothing of vital importance has been modified in the twenty odd sheets which have step by step preceded completion of the drawings of the 4-8-4 model now approaching the steam test stage. The cylinders are 3" bore and

74

3½" stroke, and Baker's valve-gear is being tried on this and the 4-6-4 express passenger engine. The disabilities of the Baker gear are well-known, but for a slide-valve engine, where it pays to keep the valve travel down – or to put it the other way round – it is an advantage not to increase the travel to the length that can be safely adopted where a more or less completely balanced valve, such as a piston-valve, can be employed without difficulty. The Baker valve-gear has been worked out so that all pins are, as far as possible, balanced; cantilevering cannot be eliminated in this gear. In addition, the angles of vibration were on the drawing, limited to 30 degrees in full gear. An accuracy in lead and port openings of within 1/100" was obtained, comparing both backward and forward gears; in the subsequent valve-setting operations, full port opening was found to be possible with 29 degrees of inclination in both directions. How wear and tear will affect the valve-gear in service has yet to be experienced. Walschaerts will be reverted to on the third machine. This gear has some advantage in the fact that all initial joint movements in the motion are (or can be) greater than those required at the valve-spindle. Exaggerated valve movements are. therefore, more easily obtained. Such movements are all that "long valve travel" means. As the writer and others have emphasised on several occasions in these columns, valve events cannot be varied except by cam-operated gears.

In the first Baker gear engine, the 4-8-4, Kayser-Ellison's ground bar case-hardening steel has been used for the important pins, and all are made to run in bushed journals. The valve-spindle has an outside guide (so easy in Baker's) to relieve the gland for the effects of angular thrusts.

The average visitor to the Kenton Miniature Railway, however, is not interested technically; he or his associates want a ride. The railway runs every Saturday, all year round, and the net proceeds have charitable objects   - at the moment, the Wembley Hospital is the recipient. Up to last season, an old English fair, of a week's duration, was held in the grounds at Kenton Grange for the benefit of local charities, and the railway, which has a continuous main line, three-quarters of a mile round, was naturally going at full capacity the whole time.

Among the voluntary helpers at the railway may be mentioned Mr. R. Beeson (of the S.M.E.E.), Messrs. S. R. Blazey, C. H. Willmot, Keniston, N. Dyer, R. Woollven, and W. A. Little. The ladies were represented by Miss C. Burns, Mrs Blazey and Miss J. Brown. Mr Elsden runs the Kenton shops under Mr. Jeffress's direction. Readers will, therefore, readily understand that Kenton's workshop activities do not finish with the building of models. Running repairs and necessary replacements figure in the many items of work to be accomplished each week.

Mr Jeffress has recently very kindly provided a piece of land for the use of the Harrow Society of Model Engineers, on which they can erect a 5", 3½" and 2½" testing track.

History of Kenton Miniature Railway

Addenda 3

Copy of letter to the Editor of the Model Engineer Magazine from W J Bassett-Lowke:

The Most Popular Gauge for Garden Railways

Dear Sir,

We were interested to read Mr R Horsfield's letter in your issue of August 30th about the above subject.

We think your correspondent will appreciate that no one gauge for garden railways could fulfil all requirements. So much depends upon the space at one's disposal, the amount of load to be carried, and also the very important question of expenditure.

We have had experience for over 20 years in garden railway construction and have built outdoor passenger carrying railways from 3½ in. gauge to 15 in. gauge, and it is our considered opinion 7¼ in. is the best gauge for the private garden railway. It is sufficiently large for the locomotive to have good wearing surfaces and to carry from 8 to 15 people according to the grades, and the radii of the curves can be kept within reasonable limits. 9½ in. gauge certainly has the advantage of being more powerful, but as this gauge is not large enough to seat two passengers abreast, it means a very long train if maximum capacity is required.

Mr. Jeffress, of Kenton Grange, who has one of the largest collections of 7¼ in. locomotives in the country, finds that this gauge excellently fulfils his garden railway requirements on his comprehensive line he is laying.

We have no hesitation in saying, from the orders we have received both at home and abroad during the past two years, that in our opinion, 7¼ in. gauge is far and away the most popular gauge for a private railway.

Locomotives of 9½ in. gauge are more scarce, because fewer have been built.

Yours faithfully,   W J Bassett-Lowke   Northampton

So the story ends for now:

Kenton Miniature Railway . . . . 1949 . . . . passed into history.

Wonderland amusements . . . . 1974 . . . . shut down.

Coniston Railway. . . . . 2012 . . . . sold

But all the seven KMR locos survive . . . . . at least until 2015.

Eric L Basire
West Moors
Dorset
March 2015

19871746R00049

Printed in Great Britain
by Amazon